ENTRIES OF THE CELL

FRANZ WRIGHT

ENTRIES OF THE CELL

MARICK PRESS
Grosse Pointe Farms, Michigan

Entries of the Cell

> *What does deep midnight have to say?*
> Nietzsche

Tell me once more how you're going to do it. I have been wondering and wondering. Tell me. By windowlight, my ghosts; by winterlight, sun seen from Pluto, handmirror of dead girl and ground-diamond desert; by taste of fresh bird blood in snow, theorem and spell. By muttering and crooning alone the same word I've been saying to reach you, forever it seems, from glad ascent to fatal fall, and all I have seasick and brainsick been trying to recall, dying to sing you, be it ever so simple and strange.

There are two infinities. Can't you see them?

Don't ask me how it works—one of star-sown space, and one of the words for it— . . .

I only know it was like living twice.

Rilke said even in prison you would still have your childhood,
incontrovertible proof he had never been anywhere near a prison.

He also said death begins at the tip of the nose, now that's
        interesting! And I am still riding the
        trains amassing corroboratory examples.

But I know something nobody taught me and I never read
        in a book.

Some people aren't even evil, they're just a disease, or its microscopic wings. Not a fatal one. Not necessarily.

Without premeditation, mindlessly, without discrimination
        they communicate themselves to anyone
        who comes within range.

It can take a long time to realize you are suffering from it.

Or to understand that you are it.

Then I saw the freeways encircling Los Angeles strangled
        with white hearses, bumper to bumper,
        moving along about 10 mph . . .

Headlights in daylight following one after another, mysterious commonplace: who has never stopped
        to let them pass

without an elongated second of identification with the absent
        person riding;

without a pang of horror,

and one of envy?

I like to light a candle after Mass, stare into the flame, and
             ask that you enter the heart of somebody
             in need of your company today.

I see you raised up, a few feet off the ground, face clenched
             no more in pain, deceased,

thin arms still outstretched to draw all men to you, and

             why can't I respond?

Even now, after ten years of more or less failing to behave
             like someone who believes, no more capable
             of maintaining a literal sense of your
             presence than I am of staring into the
             sun,

you have not left me, you have not abandoned my mind in its
             former numb and sleepless coma. And I
             know that my failure to feel you there can in
             no way diminish the fact that you are.

I light my candle, I stand a minute looking down at it, I
             ask.

Dusk-colored mountain and mountain of dusk looming
             starrily, peakless, behind it—

the mountain of *How*
I am kneeling at.

The mountain of *Why?*

There is a step to take beyond the final step.

May we ask to speak with you for a moment please, Mr.
                Wright?

I don't know, it could be the vale where souls are made, and
                then again it could be their slaughterhouse.
                Hard to tell, it is so *here* all the time—

the Eye altering alters all, it may just be one of those
                situations.

I can cry now, and do so for about 45 seconds every year
                whether I need to or not; but before the tear
                can roll all the way down my cheek it turns to
                ice, strangers

  my family became, early on. Total stranger who became my
                family—

I will die with a hammer in my hand, says the glass anvil.

And were your feelings so terrible and dark they could not
        be turned into fuel?

Refused their leaden drugs. Left and walked home, walked
        through walls, crossed the river.

Sat in a room for ten years and worked. For I left that
        gigantic locked windowless place hidden
        away in plain sight. Building without an
        address, where the speechless and
        screaming.

Oh yes, I had left that vast bed I'd been sharing with mad-
        ness's other most frequent fliers, left them
        snoring in blank black Resperidal slumber

        and through one locked ward after another
        I passed, a breeze a sixteenth of an inch
        from the floor under each of the triple
        locked doors;

goodbye metal mirror, I passed out of there. At crack of
        doom, at (gentian) dawn I left for good.

So let a certain critic smile and lift his left leg hind leg to
        piss on everything I care about and fought
        for all my life—

I left, and that was that. I must have died all at once near
        the end of a sad dream of home; or was it
        one that featured crushing and irreversible
        shame?

One featuring eyes' sentient rays, beloved eyes remembered,

voices remembered. Or one of strange brothers reunited at
        last on somebody's bookshelf—maybe

one all about how to tell, when you look back, your being
        lifted up

from your complete and mirthfully applauded annihilation.
        Or

one of the love that had promised to give back all the time
        lost for it sake. Of

the planet so alone in timeless night . . .

I walked the the length of Boston, and still the morning had
        not come.

And where was everyone?

Polaris no longer the north star.

Where is the bridge that connects the unnamable name and
        the word without world? Which is the
        bride and which the bird? What shining is
        spanned anyway—that can't be water . . .

Cross of Hiroshima ash traced on a forehead.

The black dove sent out and still out there.

I'm lying face down in bed, both arms outstretched,
        coming in low with my lights out.

That's a bunch of shit. Actually I'm here all alone in
        the dark with everyone, waiting to be
        born.

It can't be long now, and I'm really looking forward to
        inheriting the world I have heard so much
        about!

Strictly speaking, I haven't heard anything; but I have
        thought about it so much, dreamed of it
        so much.

And what an honor, to be born on earth and take my place
        among thegentle and good, the peace-loving,
        joyous and free, not to mention the
        compassionate, enlightened, incandescently
        selfless and wise.

Now I'm in a bed, I think. I'm not really that sure
        where I am, some sort of rooming house
        or lower depths rehab. I've been here for a
        while, and it is my painful duty to report, if
        anyone's still listening, our mission has run
        into some serious turbulence, to put it
        mildly.

The glaringly self-evident fact is we are only here today
        due to direct descent from the cruelest, the
        least burdened by empathy, the most covet-
        ous, greedy, and sleeplessly obsessed with
        dominance and its maintenance and

therefore, as well, the most paranoid,
puritanical, preemptively savage and
hellbent on being the last one left standing.

My idea is the law should obey us, *orphan boy tobacco. . .*

We find no evidence of those others. The more generous,
utopian and inward-looking others who
wouldnot have been doing a lot of
procreating past a certain point, seeing as
they were all dead, with the exception of a
few the slobbering and fittest morons might
have kept around to breed as slaves, or
dinner.

We have so far managed, by dint of the most arduously disci-
plined deceit, to blend in and give away none
of the horror with which we naturally
contemplate the state of things here.

To tell the honest truth, we've also thrown a couple pretty
wild parties, thanks.

This has been an extremely interesting experience, and I am
sure it has given us all a lot to think about.

Right at the moment I am sitting at a very small desk beside
a small child who can't write, doesn't draw or
play much, and has never said a single word to
anyone as far as I know.

A flawlessly beautiful child with perfect white sharp tiny
teeth, long straight blonde hair, and
profoundly dark blue eyes. A perfectly
lovely child who has no name, and is one
hundred thousand years old.

The cell will teach you all things.

There are spots in the sea, depths where light ceases to
    penetrate, a painless, dreamless and shatter-
    proof sleep holy to horrible workers: who
    will appear to replace us, after we've seem
    the Kingdom and fallen. And may they be
    as loathesome, offensive and frightening as
    possible to the literary-academic complex.

If I tell you her breasts are two small blind pink dol-
    phins who live unmolested, in eternal
    delight, in some unnamed river of South
    America,

what are you going to do about it?

And what's it about, all the dissension over God,

the word God.

The word tree has put no leaf out yet.

We were born, we supposed, knowing everything. All the
    most important words addressed to us went
    in one ear and encountering minimal resis-
    tance right out the other, but

look who was doing the addressing.

The investigations were always being led by those who'd
            most brilliantly benefited from the crime.

Northern Ohio, September '74. Nixon murders Allende.

Violet light of the wheat, we were growing old and dying
            young.

How much did we drink, how often, and why?

We drank.

When it rains, you don't ask how many raindrops fell. You

            say: it rained.

Lots of rain, many semi-colons—the cell will teach you all.

This blue world. Unattainable—stranger than
            dying,

by what unmerited grace we were allowed to come see it.

Deathrow born and bred, and yet

this blue world, stranger.

Anticipate at least a year of total unresponsive silence.

Include a stabbed self-undressed envelope, if you ever hope to see your sorry work again.

There were a couple decades when this was my primary concern.

Sadness, grieving: you will get over them, don't worry. That's the problem.

In an old notebook I have come across a dream entry from September 10th of 2000: an airliner's parked, windows dark, in the middle of a baseball field a few blocks from our house.

And look what I've come upon in *this* one leafing through these catpiss-scented, half-indecipherable and disintegrating pages.
It's a capital *F* that takes up a whole page.

My name, or grade in life?

In color a dull dead rust-red, someone's blood, and I can't imagine whose.

But never mind about that—let's take a good look at this *F.* Think about it and tell me,

who names their child *Franz* and throws him to the boys of American grade schools?

Franz. It would make a good name for a dog. Some retired
            and semi-crippled shepherd, perhaps

the great great great great great great grandson of one whose
            job was herding naked people.

He's out of work now, our friend Franz.

He's had his assignments, an occasional elderly blind man
            here, a stint on the trains there,

helping silent uniformed men hunt down ticket delinquents;

he has been seen slinking in and out of certain still-bombed
            out churches, limping along behind the pack,
            serving as some cowering junkie's skinny and
            worried-looking defence,

in the German light.

Meanwhile, here on the other side, wandering the streets this
            Franz is abruptly bashed in the shoulder by
            some very large passer-by from behind
            "Sorry," he mutters in his sleep, as he passes
            me. And "How's it going?"

An individual I do not know, like pretty close to everyone on
            earth.

And like close to everyone on earth he does not give a shit
            about how, for me, it happens to be going.

Still it's an interesting question.

The truth is I'm not feeling so good;

and to judge from their expressions neither is anyone else.

Not as bad, say, as the pregnant girl who's just been diagnosed
        with inoperable cancer, missed her train by
        seconds, and stands there alone on the
        platform in the hot stench of its wake.

Nearby the witnessing angel who shows up at all such
        events, white glare where the face is
        supposed to go, an unseeable brightness.

And how hideous he is, we would think, could we see him.

We who unreflectingly gaze every day of our lives into the
        perfectly bland face of evil, smiling back at us,
        and shaking our hands.

So far from home, messenger who has long forgotten the
        message.

Face monstrous with thirteen millions years of looking on
        and grieving,

grieving for the languageless mother keeping her distance
        and watching intently as a large doglike
        creature is eating her child, for instance;

mourning the small girl with the missing bird, vacant cage
        clutched to her chest, calling out its name,
        parents lost in the crown, the unmarked train
        cars slowing.

The other day while reading I came across the the long-
        deceased phrase *You are the love of my life*.
        I did not sneer, or bare my teeth in derision.
        I stopped a moment, leaned down, put my ear

> to it and listened, hard, because who knows
> what might not still be beating or breathing in
> there—some vividly literal meaning like *You
> personify to me the love of life* . . .

Then I remembered how long long ago I had bought it, the
>> whole illusion, everything from the most
>> remote star to the bubble of time that will burst
>> before I can finish this phrase; everything from
>> the small bloody scream of our first appearance
>> to our speechless and forsaken exit. All will be
>> forgotten, everthing you perceived, thought,
>> dreamed, hoped, remembered . . . all the past
>> all the crawling fucking coughing chest-
>> pounding nose-picking and deathward attempts
>> to make real some desperate desire, like
>> standing upright for a minute in the sun. The
>> sun that will die.

First walker, seafarer, spacefarer—where did it start,
>> how, and why? Show me the first to form
>> word, the first to weep, the first to sing. The
>> first to kill not others but himself. The first to
>> die for someone else.

A member of our species wrote *Love, which moves the sun
>> and other stars,* and saw it animating all that is.

And the darkness has neither overwhelmed nor
>> comprehended it,

yet.

Love. Of all thing least illusory.

Love which whispers *It's very simple: what you long for,*
                provide.

Let's say that five a.m. arrives and finds you fully dressed in
                yesterday's clothes,

the clock set for six.

It's bad, no question about it, and yet.

What a relief it will be, won't it—stumbling out once more
                to see the morning street with its familiar
                million strangers streaming past, you standing
                there watching them part with blind eyes
                around you on either side, God bless them,
                every one, everyone who's not going to hurt
                you today, all the strangers, how you love
                them all at once, how close you feel to them.

Because the soul is a stranger in this world.

for Fady Joudah

NOTE

"The cell will teach you all things" is a saying attributed to one of the Christian desert Fathers, the abbot Moses the Ethiopian, d.c. 375.

"Lots of rain, many semi-colons . . ." is a phrase written by John Cheerver, in all his brilliance, in the diary he kept while he was going through detoxification from alcohol.

"Because the soul is a stranger in this world," the final line of the poem, is a fairly literal translation of a sentence in Heidegger.

For unknown reasons I was assisted in the writing of this poem by the spirit of John Lennon's book *In His Own Write,* which first appeared in 1964.

ISBN: 978-1-934851-29-6

Cover art by Elizabeth Oehlkers Wright

Printed in the United States

MARICK PRESS
P.O. Box 36253
Grosse Pointe Farms
Michigan 48236
www.marickpress.com

www.ingramcontent.com/pod-product-compliance
Lightning Source LLC
LaVergne TN
LVHW012058090426
835512LV00033B/388